ARCADE ARTHUR MEETS MARVELLOUS MARTHA

Clive Gifford

Illustrated by Mike McLester

The Star Games Arcade was the best by far. It had a burger bar and hard games like Kart Park. Children gathered around Arthur as he played Kart Park.

He was fairly new at the arcade, but he had become a star. He steered and changed gears like he had raced karts forever. His kart darted over the line in a new record time. How clever!

Everyone cheered Arthur as his time made him number one. Someone cried, "Arcade Arthur, well done!"

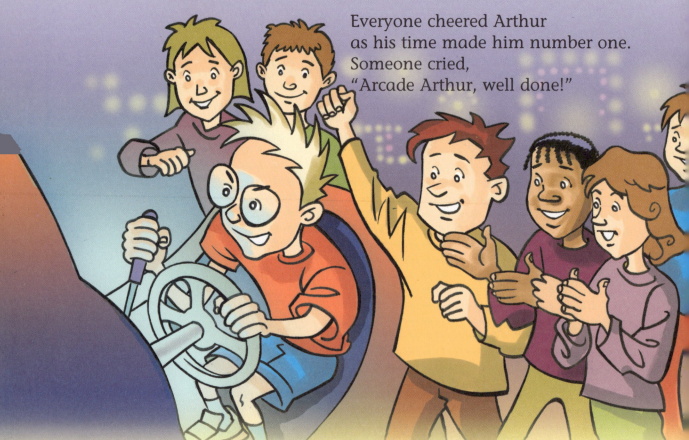

Arthur tried to shrug off the cheers of **"Arcade Arthur! Arcade Arthur!"** but secretly he was very proud to be the best player there. "Never fear, Arcade Arthur's here," he said, boastfully.

Can you work out whether to add **er** or **re** to the end of the following letters to make new words?

play er

ca re

fla re

de er

sta re

ste er

cent re

few er

clev er

prepa re

"Sorry to alarm you, Arthur," said a girl with ginger hair. "But all that cheering should be for the other star here. She's called Marvellous Martha, and she's far better than you."

Some of the other players nodded and one said, "That's true. She has a flair for driver games, and space games like Warp Crew."

"Where is she?" said Arthur, feeling rather startled.

"She's here, right in front of you," said the girl. "I'm Martha!"

"But I'm the expert on Iceberg Alert and Kart Park," snarled Arthur.

"Not on Iceberg Alert," smirked Martha. "Not any longer!"

After Martha left, Arthur checked the highest scores and tore at his hair. His name was nowhere. Only Martha's name was there.

Many names of people and objects have shortened forms. For example, Arthur can become Art. Write out in full each of these shortened names of people and objects.

People

Dan Daniel

Sue Suezan

Dave David

Jo Joseph

Ed Edmund

Objects

phone Telephone

bike bicycle

telly television

plane aeroplane

fridge refride

Arthur and Martha had got off to a bad start and it got far, far worse the next time they were in the arcade.
Martha tripped over a power lead near Arthur, by mistake.
He was playing Prairie Scare before a tea break.

In Prairie Scare, the aim was to get the farm's harvest into the barn.
You had to be smart and alert to stop it coming to harm.

Arthur was doing ever so well –
he was near to a perfect score –
but the power went off, making him despair.

Martha said, "Sorry,"
and her face went as red as her hair.

"You dirty **cheater**!"
snarled angry Arthur.
"How dare you!
Clear off, Martha, and beware!"

Write eer, ere, ear, are or air in each space to make a word which fits the sentence.

Everyone ch__eer__ed Arthur as his time made him number one.

She has a fl_____ for driver games.

"Never f__air__, Arcade Arthur's h_____."

"She turned off the power to Pr__are__ie Sc__are__."

He searched h_____, th_____ and everywh_____.

He was f_____ly new at the arcade, but he had become a star.

His name was nowh__ere__. Only Martha's name was th_____.

"Oh d__ear__, I f_____ my _____s really are h_____ing this," sighed Carl.

7

Arthur's anger got greater, the longer he stayed in the arcade. Then he did something you should never do. He waited until Martha nearly had a high score on Kart Park, then jerked her steering wheel to make her kart crash.

Martha jerked the steering wheel back and swerved over the line. Even with nearly crashing her kart, she had the fastest-ever time!

"**A r r r r h**, there, there, cry baby," jeered Martha. "Serves you right for playing such a dirty trick, Arthur!"

Arthur saw Martha's high score and glared at her.

"I can't bear you, you twerp!" he declared.

"At least I don't cheat, you nerd!" Martha jeered.

An apostrophe, ', can be used to show that some letters are missing when a phrase is shortened. For example, I am becomes I'm. Draw lines to match the words which mean the same thing.

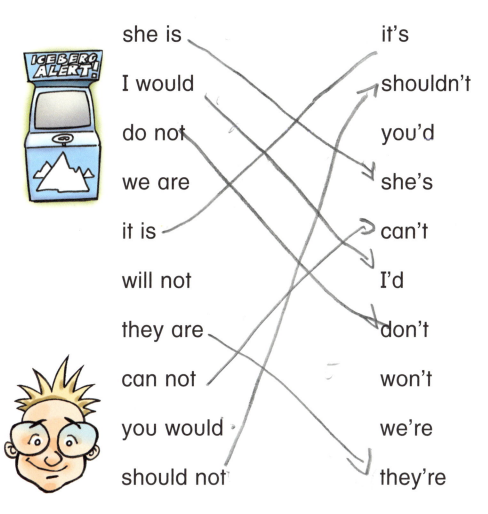

she is	it's
I would	shouldn't
do not	you'd
we are	she's
it is	can't
will not	I'd
they are	don't
can not	won't
you would	we're
should not	they're

Carl, the owner of the arcade, stepped out of his office. "Arcade Arthur, Marvellous Martha, there's no need to argue. You are both superstars, the best in my arcade by far."

"She started it," snarled Arthur. "She turned off the power to Prairie Scare. That's unfair!"

"It was an accident. I didn't mean any harm," said Martha. "And what about you jerking my steering wheel on Kart Park?"

"Oh dear, I fear my ears really are hearing this," sighed Carl. "Your arguing is scaring the younger players in my arcade."

"I don't want to bar you, but will you pair ever stop arguing?"

Arthur and Martha both shook their heads firmly. **"Never!"**

This computer game has a virus which has removed all of the punctuation marks and capital letters from this screen of instructions. Can you put everything back?

Use
11 capital letters   5 full stops (.)   2 commas (,)
3 apostrophes (')   1 question mark (?)   1 exclamation mark (!)

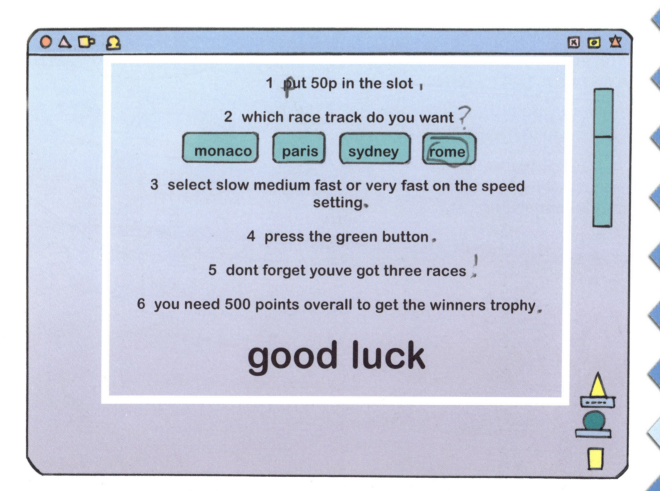

1 put 50p in the slot,

2 which race track do you want?
   monaco   paris   sydney   rome

3 select slow medium fast or very fast on the speed setting.

4 press the green button.

5 dont forget youve got three races!

6 you need 500 points overall to get the winners trophy.

good luck

Carl led the pair into a large, dark area, painted red. "Let's see how you two fare in the Tower of Power," he said.

"The aim of this game is to make the players a **team**," explained Carl.

"Climb the tower's stairs to get to the arch, but beware!

Falling squares take your power, and may knock you off the stairs.

If either of you falls into the sewer river below, you both lose.

If you're smart, you'll share the work, but I'll leave you to choose."

Carl left, and the pair were startled by the sudden glare of bright lights. They found themselves staring at real stairs, a real arch and a real river.

This was no regular arcade game, not with those real large squares, falling from the tower roof, high above the stairs.

A simile is a phrase that describes something by comparing it with something else. See if you can finish off these common similes.

as strong as __bull__

as cold as __ice__

as wise as __an owl__

as light as __a feather__

as brave as __a lion__

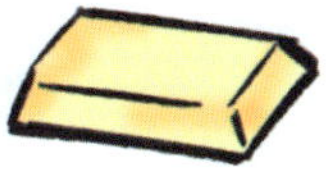

as hard as __gold__

as good as _____

as slippery as _____

as slow as _____

as cunning as _____

At first, Arthur and Martha found the Tower of Power easy to play. The squares fell slowly and the pair could sway out of their way.

"It's so easy, even you can do it," sneered Martha, passing Arthur.

"Phew, that terrible smell is giving me a fever," swooned Martha. The sewer river below smelt of garbage and farmyards.

"Smells as bad as you," sneered Arthur, barging past Martha.

"Charming," snarled Martha. "**Look out**, over there!"

Arthur laughed just as he was hit by a large, scarlet square. It didn't hurt, but it made him feel tired and hungry. Martha was also hit and lost lots of her energy too.

After being hit by more squares, the pair felt starving.

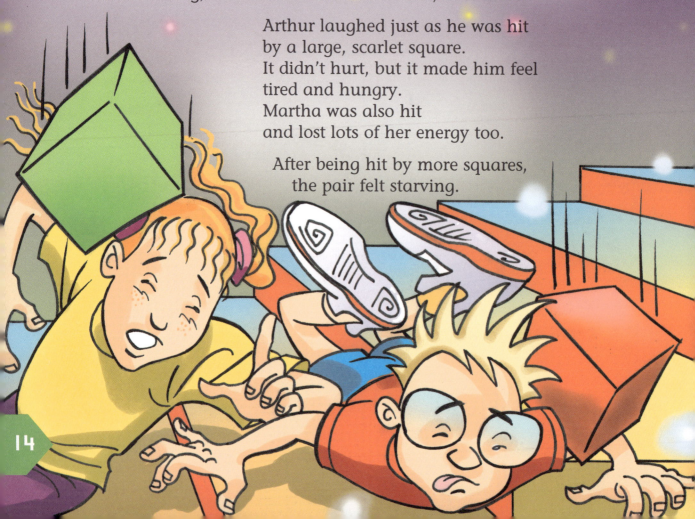

Here are some of the computer games at the Star Games Arcade. Use **ar**, **er** and **ur** to fill in the gaps and complete the names.

K a r t
P a r k

Iceb e r g
Al e r t
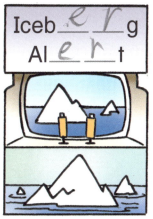

Prairie
Sc a r e

Thund e r
C a r s

Ast e r oid
B u r n
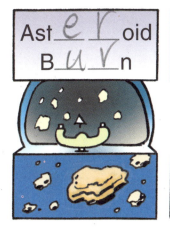

W ___ p
Crew

St a r
Fev e r

F a r m
Al ___ m

"When this is over, we'll both need a square meal!" Arthur joked weakly.

"Ha, ha," sneered Martha. "We're in danger," she added bleakly.

Arthur stared upwards at the large numbers of falling squares and saw that between them and the arch stood many stairs.

"Do you remember Carl said to share the work?" asked Martha. "If we barge into each other and fall into the river, it's game over."

Arthur darted out of the way of another square and thought about their task. "So we have to be smart and work together?" he asked.

"Afraid so," said Martha. "It's the only way to play."

Martha offered her hand and Arthur shook it hard. They would work together to reach the sparkling arch.

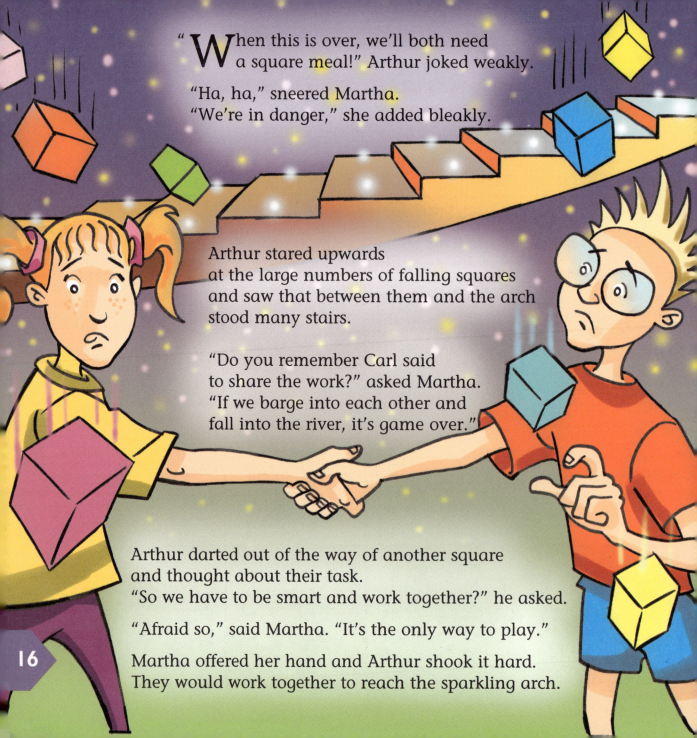

Can you add **air**, **er** or **ar** to either the start or the end of the following groups of letters to make a word? Watch out for the last one, which needs letters added both at the start and the end.

_ar_cade

furth_er_

_ar_gue

comput_er_

fl_air_

_ar_tist

____ror

aft____

li____

_ar_mch_air_

17

Arthur and Martha marched up the Tower of Power. One darted up a stair, whilst the other barged the squares.

"Watch out, Arthur!" screamed Martha, as a square blasted past.

Martha charged across and helped Arthur swerve clear. "Thanks, Martha … Behind you!" cried Arthur.

Martha jerked her head, but she was hit by a large square. She started to fall, as Arthur charged down some stairs.

He grabbed Martha's hand just in time.

"Thanks, Arthur, you're a **lifesaver**!" said Martha.

"No bother. Like you said, we have to work together," he replied.

Tired but cheerful, the pair reached the sparkling arch.

Synonyms are words which have the same or similar meanings. Antonyms are words which mean the opposite of each other. Can you find a synonym and an antonym for each word?

filthy fearless ancient loser champion harmless wealthy nearer
clean poor simple dangerous further complex cowardly young

	Synonym	Antonym
old		
easy		
rich		
closer		
dirty		
winner		
brave		
harmful		

Martha and Arthur got a surprise on the other side of the arch. They found themselves back in the arcade, in the burger bar.

Carl cheered, "Well done, Marvellous Martha and Arcade Arthur!" He asked, "So who was the winner? Was it you Martha?"

"No," said Martha. "Arthur's the **expert**."

"No, Martha was better," argued Arthur. "She was ever so **alert**."

"Aha, you are both winners," beamed Carl. "Here is your prize."

He handed Arthur and Martha a pair of very large burgers.

"Time for my Superstar Burgers to repair your energy levels. Then you can try my super dairy cream dessert!"

Arthur and Martha happily shared the burgers and dessert. It was all superb!

Now you have read the story of Arthur, Martha and the Star Games Arcade, see if you can answer all of these questions.

1. What game was Arthur playing at the start of the story? _____

2. What was the full name of the arcade in which Arthur and Martha played? _____

3. What game was Arthur playing when the power went off? _____

4. What was the name of the owner of the arcade? _____

5. What bad thing did Arthur do whilst Martha played Kart Park? _____

6. What was the colour of the first square to hit Arthur? _____

7. What was the name of the real-life game Martha and Arthur played? _____

8. Which place did Martha and Arthur have to reach to complete the game? _____

9. Who first offered their hand to shake on a deal to work together? _____

Answers

Page 3

player
care
flare
deer
stare
steer
centre
fewer
clever
prepare

Page 5

Many variations are possible:
Daniel
Susan
David
Joanne
Edward
telephone
bicycle
television
aeroplane
refrigerator

Page 7

Everyone ch<u>ee</u>red Arthur as his time made him number one.
She has a fl<u>air</u> for driver games.
"Never f<u>ear</u>, Arcade Arthur's h<u>ere</u>."
"She turned off the power to Pr<u>air</u>ie Sc<u>are</u>."
He searched h<u>ere</u>, th<u>ere</u> and everywh<u>ere</u>.
He was f<u>air</u>ly new at the arcade, but he had become a star.
His name was nowh<u>ere</u>. Only Martha's name was th<u>ere</u>.
"Oh d<u>ear</u>, I f<u>ear</u> my <u>ear</u>s really are h<u>ear</u>ing this," sighed Carl.

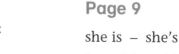

Page 9

she is – she's
I would – I'd
do not – don't
we are – we're
it is – it's
will not – won't
they are – they're
can not – can't
you would – you'd
should not – shouldn't

Page 11

1 Put 50p in the slot.
2 Which race track do you want?
   Monaco
   Paris
   Sydney
   Rome
3 Select slow, medium, fast or very fast on the speed setting.
4 Press the green button.
5 Don't forget you've got three races.
6 You need 500 points overall to get the winner's trophy.
Good luck!

Page 13

as strong as an ox
as cold as ice
as wise as an owl
as light as a feather
as brave as a lion
as hard as nails
as good as gold
as slippery as a snake
as slow as a snail
as cunning as a fox

Page 15

Kart Park
Iceberg Alert
Prairie Scare
Thunder Cars
Asteroid Burn
Warp Crew
Star Fever
Farm Alarm

Page 17

arcade   computer   error   armchair
further   flair   after
argue   artist   liar

Page 19

	Synonym	Antonym
old	ancient	young
easy	simple	complex
rich	wealthy	poor
closer	nearer	further
dirty	filthy	clean
winner	champion	loser
brave	fearless	cowardly
harmful	dangerous	harmless

Page 21

1. Kart Park
2. The Star Games Arcade
3. Prairie Scare
4. Carl
5. he jerked Martha's steering wheel
6. scarlet
7. The Tower of Power
8. the sparkling arch
9. Martha

Published 2005

Letts Educational, The Chiswick Centre,
414 Chiswick High Road, London W4 5TF
Tel 020 8996 3333   Fax 020 8996 8390
Email mail@lettsed.co.uk
www.letts-education.com

Text, design and illustrations © Letts Educational Ltd 2005
Nelson handwriting font © Thomas Nelson

Book Concept, Development and Series Editor:
Helen Jacobs, Publishing Director
Author: Clive Gifford
Book Design: 2idesign ltd, Cambridge
Illustrations: Mike McLester, The Bright Agency

Letts Educational Limited is a division of Granada Learning.
Part of Granada plc.
All rights reserved. No part of this publication may be reproduced, stored in a retrieval system, or transmitted, in any form or by any means, electronic, mechanical, photocopying, recording or otherwise, without the prior permission of Letts Educational.

British Library Cataloguing in Publication Data

A CIP record for this book is available from the British Library.

ISBN 1 84315 490 0

Printed in Italy

Colour reproduction by PDQ Digital Media Solutions Ltd, Bungay, Suffolk NR35 1BY